GREG LUZINSKI
LEFT FIELDER
PHILADELPHIA
PHILLIES

RICHIE ASHBURN
CENTER FIELDER
PHILADELPHIA
PHILLIES

THE STORY OF THE PHILADELPHIA PHILLIES

Published by Creative Education
P.O. Box 227, Mankato, Minnesota 56002
Creative Education is an imprint of The Creative Company
www.thecreativecompany.us

Design and production by Blue Design
Art direction by Rita Marshall
Printed by Corporate Graphics in the United States of America

Photographs by Getty Images (Dan Bigelow, Chicago History Museum, Diamond Images, Focus on Sport, Drew Hallowell, Jed Jacobsohn, Mitchell Layton, Robert Leiter/MLB Photos, Bob Levey, National Baseball Hall of Fame Library/MLB Photos, Rich Pilling/MLB Photos, Louis Requena/MLB Photos, George Silk/ Time & Life Pictures, Rick Stewart, Tony Tomsic/MLB Photos, Rob Tringali/Sportschrome, Ron Vesely/ MLB Photos)

Library of Congress Cataloging-in-Publication Data

Goodman, Michael E.
The story of the Philadelphia Phillies / by Michael E. Goodman.
p. cm. — (Baseball: the great American game)
Includes index.
Summary: The history of the Philadelphia Phillies professional baseball team from its inaugural 1883 season to today, spotlighting the team's greatest players and most memorable moments.
ISBN 978-1-60818-051-6
1. Philadelphia Phillies (Baseball team)—History—Juvenile literature. I. Title. II. Series.

GV875.P45G66 2010
796.357'640974811—dc22   2010025213

CPSIA: 110310 PO1381

First Edition
9 8 7 6 5 4 3 2 1

Page 3: Right fielder Sam Thompson
Page 4: Second baseman Chase Utley

BASEBALL: THE GREAT AMERICAN GAME

THE STORY
OF THE
PHILADELPHIA
PHILLIES

Michael E. Goodman

CREATIVE EDUCATION

CONTENTS

HISTORIC ROOTS

In 1643, Sweden established a colony on America's mid-Atlantic coast that later came under Dutch and then British control. American Indians called the heavily wooded area *Coaquannok*, which means "grove of tall pine trees." After William Penn arrived as governor of the British colony in 1682, the area was renamed Pennsylvania ("Penn's woods"). There, Penn and his fellow Quakers—members of a Christian religious order—established a city they called Philadelphia. The name was a Greek word meaning "brotherly love," as the city's founders hoped Philadelphia would become a model for religious tolerance in the New World.

Philadelphia quickly grew in size and importance, and it was there, in 1776, that America declared its independence from Great Britain. Exactly 100 years later, in 1876, Philadelphia became the home of one of the first professional baseball teams in the young National League (NL)—the Athletics. Although that club soon folded due to financial woes, it was replaced in 1883 by a franchise that still exists today. Owner

Philadelphia's architecture reflects its rich history, with centuries-old buildings standing alongside modern skyscrapers in the city's downtown district.

PITCHER · STEVE CARLTON

Pittsburgh Pirates Hall-of-Famer Willie Stargell once said, "Hitting against Steve Carlton was like trying to sip coffee through a fork." Carlton's slider was just that frustrating for batters to make contact with as they watched it dip out of reach. "Lefty" was the most dominant left-handed pitcher of his era; in fact, only one left-hander in baseball history (Warren Spahn) won more games than Carlton, and only two pitchers (Roger Clemens and Randy Johnson) won more Cy Young Awards. A demanding training regimen that included martial arts techniques made Carlton one of the most physically fit—and intimidating—players of his time.

STEVE CARLTON
PITCHER

PHILADELPHIA PHILLIES

STATS

Phillies seasons: 1972–86

Height: 6-foot-4

Weight: 210

- **4,136 career strikeouts**

- **10-time All-Star**

- **4-time Cy Young Award winner**

- **Baseball Hall of Fame inductee (1994)**

A. J. Reach wanted to call that team the Athletics also, but the name had been grabbed by a club in another league. So he called his team the Philadelphias, or "Phillies" for short.

The Phillies played their first professional game on May 1, 1883, at Recreation Park in front of 1,200 fans. They lost a close battle to the Providence Grays that day, 4–3. It was the first of 81 losses they would suffer that season while winning only 17 games. The next year, however, future Hall-of-Famer Harry Wright took over as manager and began building a consistent winner in Philadelphia.

The club's first star was pitcher Charlie Ferguson, who won 99 games in the 4 years from 1884 to 1887 and then tragically died of typhoid fever when he was only 25. Other top hurlers included pint-sized William "Kid" Gleason, who won 38 games in 1890—still a club record—while also spending some time at second base, and right-hander Gus Weyhing, who won 32 times in 1892. The team's early offensive standouts were hard-hitting outfielder/first baseman Ed Delahanty, whose batting average topped the .400 mark 3 times in the 1890s, and muscular outfielder Sam Thompson, whose 20 home runs in 1889 were

the fifth-most in league history up to that time.

By the early 1900s, the Phillies had acquired a reputation as a strong hitting team with weak pitching. They could put up a lot of runs but more often than not were outscored by their opponents. That reputation began to change when a tall, gangly pitcher named Grover Cleveland Alexander joined the team in 1911. In his rookie year, "Alexander the Great" led the league in wins (28), complete games (31), and shutouts (7). "He could pitch into a tin can," said sportswriter Grantland Rice. "His control was always remarkable—the finest I have ever seen."

In 1915, Alexander and his teammates won 90 games and earned the franchise's first NL pennant. Alexander had an amazing year, going 31–10 and leading the league with a 1.22 earned-run average (ERA) and 241 strikeouts. Outfielder Gavvy Cravath smacked a club-record 24 home runs, while first baseman Fred Luderus finished second in the league batting race with a .315 average. In the 1915 World Series, the Phillies fell quickly to the Boston Red Sox, who were led by star pitcher and slugger Babe Ruth. Philadelphia would not play in another World Series for 35 years.

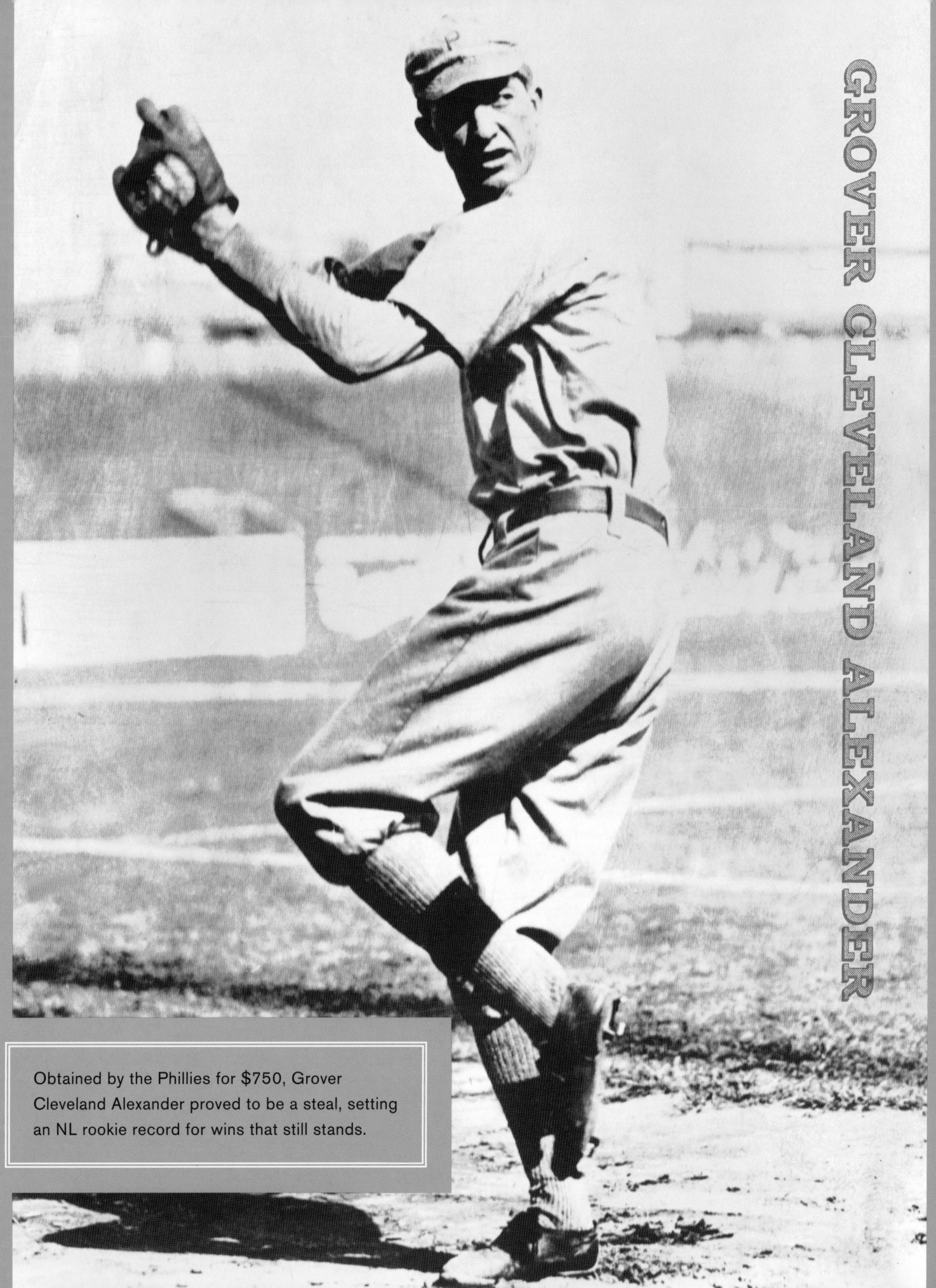

GROVER CLEVELAND ALEXANDER

Obtained by the Phillies for $750, Grover Cleveland Alexander proved to be a steal, setting an NL rookie record for wins that still stands.

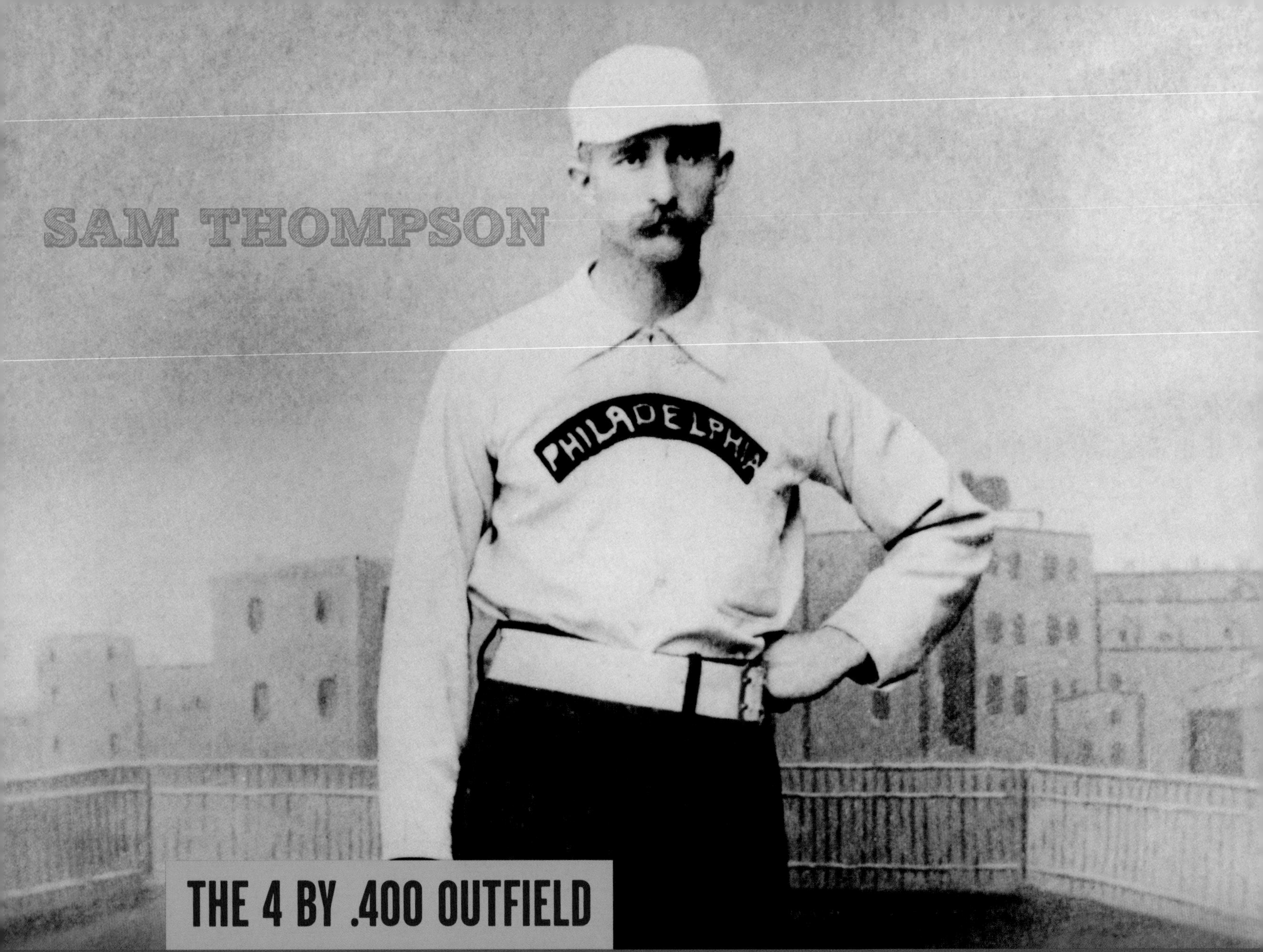

SAM THOMPSON

THE 4 BY .400 OUTFIELD

You may have heard of a 4 by 400-meter relay team in track, but have you ever heard of a 4 by .400 outfield? That's when a baseball team's three starters and top substitute all bat over .400 for the season. The 1894 Philadelphia Phillies had just such an outfield. The three starters were all future Hall-of-Famers— Sam Thompson, Ed Delahanty, and Billy Hamilton. Respectively, they batted .415, .404, and .403 that year. The key reserve was Tuck Turner, who hit .418 in 82 games. The rest of the team that season did its share of hitting, too. All eight Phillies regulars batted over .298 for the year, and the team's overall batting average was an amazing .350, still an all-time major-league record. Yet even with all that firepower, the Phillies finished fourth in the NL in 1894, 18 games behind the first-place Baltimore Orioles. The problem was that the club's pitching staff ranked 10th among the 12 NL teams and gave up nearly 6 earned runs per game, losing games by such high-scoring totals as 20–10, 19–9, and 18–14. The hard-hitting 1894 Phillies began an unfortunate tradition in Philadelphia of teams that were "all hit, no pitch."

CATCHER · BOB BOONE

The best word to describe Bob Boone was "durable." He was the first catcher in major-league history to play more than 2,000 games behind the plate, and his 2,225 total games were a record later broken by Chicago White Sox backstop Carlton Fisk in 1993. Although he was known more for his defense than his offense, Boone led the Phillies in batting during their 1980 World Series triumph, hitting .412 while catching every inning of all six games. He was the son of major-league shortstop Ray Boone and the father of two major-leaguers (infielders Bret and Aaron Boone).

BOB BOONE
CATCHER

PHILADELPHIA
PHILLIES

STATS

Phillies seasons: 1972–81

Height: 6-foot-2

Weight: 202

- **826 career RBI**

- **4-time All-Star**

- **7-time Gold Glove winner**

- **142 career sacrifice bunts**

PHILLIES

FIRST BASEMAN · RYAN HOWARD

On the field, Ryan Howard was big and powerful, with a fiercely competitive spirit and a mighty swing. But off the field, he was quiet and gentle—the Phillies' silent leader. Howard burst onto the scene in Philadelphia in 2005 and set major-league records by reaching 100, 150, and 200 career home runs more quickly than any other player in history. The secret to Howard's success at the plate and in the field was hard work. "I'm always working on everything," he said. "Offense, defense, speed, agility—I'm always trying to get as close to perfect as possible."

STATS

Phillies seasons: 2004–present

Height: 6-foot-4

Weight: 260

- **253 career HR**
- **748 career RBI**
- **2005 NL Rookie of the Year**
- **2006 NL MVP**

RYAN HOWARD
FIRST BASEMAN

PHILADELPHIA
PHILLIES

THE PITCHING CURSE

L ed by Alexander's 33 wins in 1916 and 30 in 1917, the Phillies finished second in the NL both years. Then, before the 1918 season, financial problems forced team owner Bill Baker to sell his star to the Chicago Cubs. It was a turning point for the franchise—and not for the better. After Alexander left, a curse seemed to come over the team's pitching staff. No Phillies pitcher would win 20 or more games in a season for the next 31 years.

Phillies teams continued to hit the ball well and with power during the 1920s behind standout outfielders Fred Leach, a career .300 hitter, and Cy Williams, a powerful dead-pull hitter. They scored runs in bunches, but their pitchers usually gave up even more. As a result, the Phillies finished at or near the bottom of the NL each season.

In 1930, Philadelphia set new records as an "all hit, no pitch" team. That year, all eight Phillies regulars batted .280 or better, led by slugging outfielders Chuck Klein at .386 and Francis "Lefty" O'Doul at .383. The Phils' powerful offense was sabotaged by horrible pitching, however, and the team finished in the NL cellar, an astonishing 40 games behind the league-leading St. Louis Cardinals. "That was the best-hitting rotten team I had ever seen," noted Cubs outfielder Hack Wilson.

Little by little, Phillies fans started to desert the team, and the club's owners lost money. Top players were sold or traded away for lesser players who could be paid lower salaries. Things got so bad that the league had to take over the debt-ridden team in 1943 and find new owners. It was then that wealthy businessman Bob Carpenter and his family came forward to purchase the club.

The new owners invested money in building up the Phillies' minor-league system. Within five years, such future stars as speedy outfielder Richie Ashburn, slick-fielding shortstop Granny Hamner, and hard-throwing pitcher Robin Roberts were brought up to Philadelphia. The young, hungry Phils began a dramatic rise in the standings, going from last place in 1947 to third place in 1949. Fans began calling their youthful heroes the "Whiz Kids" and dreaming of another pennant.

Leading the 1950 Phillies team was a pair of very different pitchers: Roberts, a young fireballer, and Jim Konstanty, a wily veteran reliever

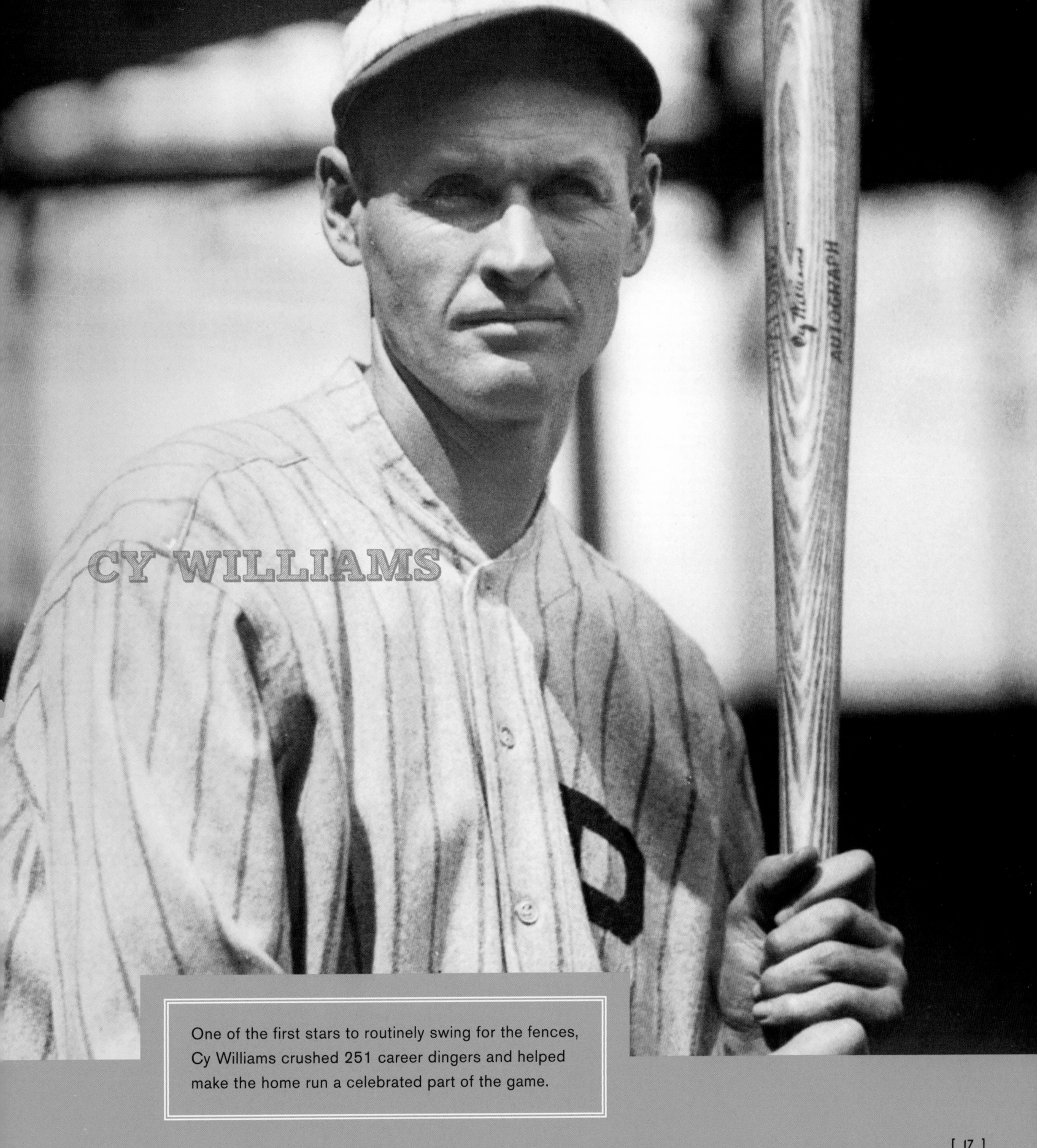

CY WILLIAMS

One of the first stars to routinely swing for the fences, Cy Williams crushed 251 career dingers and helped make the home run a celebrated part of the game.

SECOND BASEMAN · TONY TAYLOR

Phillies fans could be certain of one thing during the 1960s—that Tony Taylor would be in the lineup as the team's second baseman nearly every game. The fans loved Taylor for his hustle and his constant smile. On offense, the Cuban-born infielder was a contact hitter with little power. Still, he recorded more than 2,000 hits in his career. Where Taylor really excelled, though, was in the field. During the 1963 season, for example, he played 157 games at second and third base and committed only 10 fielding errors. In 2004, he was inducted into the Hispanic Heritage Baseball Museum Hall of Fame.

TONY TAYLOR
SECOND BASEMAN

PHILADELPHIA
PHILLIES

STATS

Phillies seasons: 1960–71, 1974–76

Height: 5-foot-9

Weight: 180

• **2,007 career hits**

• **86 career triples**

• **234 career stolen bases**

• **1960 All-Star**

famous for his tantalizing changeups. Konstanty was one of baseball's first closers. In 1950, he made 74 end-of-game appearances, won 16 games, and saved 22—feats that earned him NL Most Valuable Player (MVP) honors.

Still, it was Roberts who was the Phils' most important pitching weapon in 1950 and for many years afterward. Roberts went 20–11 in 1950, the first of 6 straight seasons in which he won 20 or more games. Roberts was a one-of-a-kind competitor. Some opponents thought he was downright nasty, but, mostly, Roberts just hated to lose. "I never slept after I lost," he said. "I'd see those base hits over and over in my mind, and they would drive me crazy."

During his Hall of Fame career, Roberts won 286 games. But no win was more important than the 10-inning victory he earned on the last day of the 1950 season against the Brooklyn Dodgers, as that victory clinched the Phillies' first pennant in 35 years. The New York Yankees swept Philadelphia in the 1950 World Series, but the loss took nothing away from the magic created by the Whiz Kids that year.

THE PHILADELPHIA BLUE JAYS

Have the Phillies always been called the Phillies? Officially, yes. No other NL team has had the same name as long as the Phillies. However, the club has had two unofficial nicknames. Some writers called the team the "Quakers" between 1883 and 1889, but that name never stuck. Then, in 1943, when the Carpenter family took over the nearly bankrupt franchise, they decided to hold a contest for a new team name. Thousands of entries poured in. Some sarcastic fans suggested "Stinkers" or "Duds," since the team had lost 100 or more games for 5 straight seasons. One fan suggested "Yankees," hoping that the New York Yankees' luck would rub off on Philadelphia's team. The winning entry was "Blue Jays." As a result, for the next two seasons, the team's uniforms were changed from bright red to dark blue and white (though the club's official name was never altered). The changes didn't improve the club's performance on the field, though. After two unsuccessful seasons as Blue Jays, the decision was made to resume calling the team the Phillies and return to the traditional red look. Phillies history ran into the Blue Jays name again some 50 years later when Philadelphia met Toronto in the 1993 World Series.

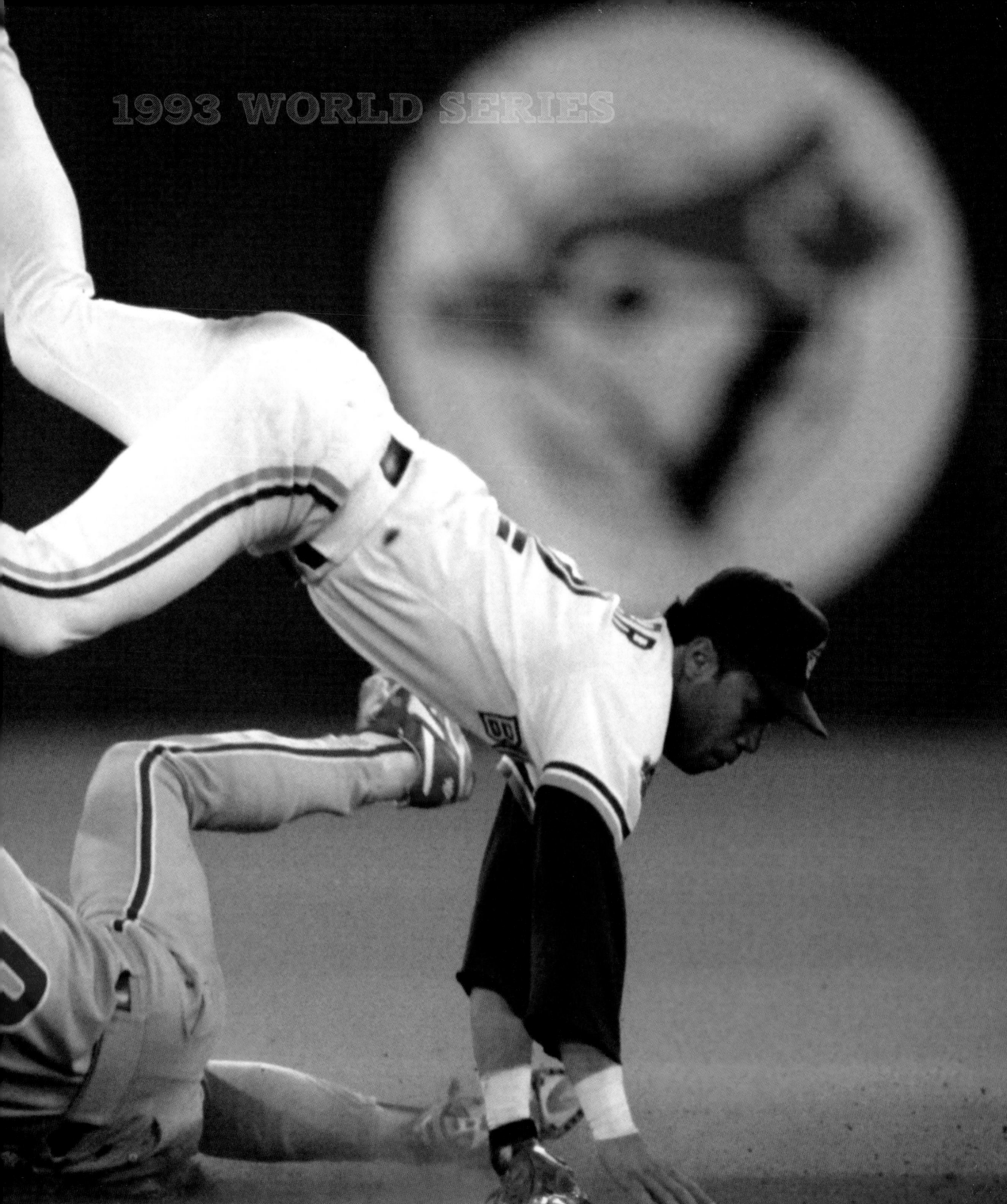

FROM BOTTOM TO TOP

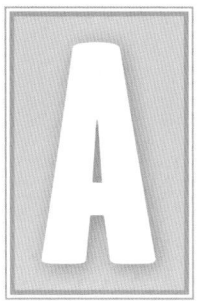fter their 1950 title run, the Phillies sank back in the NL standings. Highlights of the decade included 2 NL batting titles by Ashburn (in 1955 and 1958) and the run-generating exploits of slugging outfielder Del Ennis, who posted 100 or more runs batted in (RBI) 5 times from 1950 to 1955. Roberts continued to shine on the mound and was supported by hard-throwing right-hander Jack Sanford.

The club showed improvement going into the 1960s and made another run at the NL pennant in 1964 under manager Gene Mauch. Led by sidearming righty Jim Bunning and rookie third baseman Dick Allen, the team was in first place by 6 and a half games with only 12 games to go. Then the club suffered what became known in Philadelphia as "The Phold." (That's "fold" spelled with a *ph*, as in "Phillies.") Philadelphia lost 10 straight games and ended the season 1 game behind St. Louis. The Phold would haunt Phillies fans for many years.

The NL was split into two divisions in 1969, and the Phillies were placed in the Eastern Division. The club's physical location also

THIRD BASEMAN · MIKE SCHMIDT

Some major-league third basemen are known for hitting homers and driving in runs. Others are noted for their quick reflexes and great range in the field. Mike Schmidt was famous for both his bat and glove. He led the NL in home runs a record 8 seasons and was awarded 10 Gold Gloves. One of the main reasons for his success was his strong work ethic. "I enjoyed the pre-game preparation each day more than the game," he once said. During his 18 seasons in Philadelphia, Schmidt helped transform the Phillies from the league's doormat into one of its most dominant teams.

MIKE SCHMIDT
THIRD BASEMAN

PHILADELPHIA
PHILLIES

STATS

Phillies seasons: 1972–89

Height: 6-foot-2

Weight: 205

- 548 career HR

- 12-time All-Star

- 3-time NL MVP

- Baseball Hall of Fame inductee (1995)

BEFORE "THE PHOLD"

The 1964 Phillies are usually remembered simply for The Phold—when the team collapsed in the last two weeks of the season and lost the NL pennant. But the Phillies experienced many happy moments that season, with the most significant occurring on Father's Day, when Jim Bunning, a father of seven, tossed a perfect game against the Mets in New York. Bunning threw just 90 pitches that day, and 79 of them were strikes; he never came close to issuing a walk. When the tension was building in the ninth inning, Bunning called catcher Gus Triandos to the mound. What did they talk about?

Bunning asked Triandos to tell him a joke. The two had a quick laugh, and then Bunning completed his gem. Bunning led the Phillies with 19 wins in 1964, his first year playing in Philadelphia. Another newcomer—rookie third baseman Dick Allen—also gave Phillies fans reason to cheer in 1964. He batted .318, with 29 homers and 91 RBI, and was named the NL Rookie of the Year. Outfielder Johnny Callison was also an award-winner that season, earning All-Star Game MVP honors when his three-run walk-off homer in the ninth inning powered the NL squad to victory.

changed in 1971, when it moved from Connie Mack Stadium into Veterans Stadium. Sound reverberated inside the circular, seven-level structure, enhancing the crowd noise and intimidating opponents. Soon, those crowds had more reasons to make noise. In 1972, two future Hall-of-Famers joined the Phillies: strikeout ace pitcher Steve "Lefty" Carlton and strongman third baseman Mike Schmidt. Building around these players, the Phillies put together a squad that finally featured outstanding pitching and power in equal measures.

Carlton was an intense and private player. Lefty hated to talk to fans or sportswriters; instead, he let his excellent fastball and exploding slider do all the talking for him. Those 2 pitches helped him win 27 games in 1972—a year the Phils won only 59 games—and the first of his 4 Cy Young Awards as the league's best pitcher.

Schmidt, the team's main power source during the 1970s and '80s, was considered by many people to be the best all-around third baseman in baseball history. During his 18-year career with the Phillies, "Schmitty" slammed 548 home runs and drove in 1,595 runs. He also earned nine straight Gold Glove awards as the league's best-fielding

Greg Luzinksi led the NL with 120 RBI in 1975 and then increased that total to 130 in 1977.

third-sacker. *The Sporting News* named Schmidt its "Baseball Player of the 1980s," and Philadelphia fans elected him the "Greatest Phillies Player Ever" in 1983. There was no secret to Schmidt's greatness—it was based on hard work. "If you could measure time and effort put in to succeed on the baseball field by dirt on your uniform," he once said, "mine would be black."

The Phils of the late 1970s and early '80s had other stars, too. They included intense relief pitcher Tug McGraw, muscle-bound outfielder Greg "The Bull" Luzinski, durable catcher Bob Boone, and fiery shortstop Larry Bowa. These players led the club to three NL East championships in a row from 1976 to 1978, though the Phillies were eliminated in the NL Championship Series (NLCS) each year. Then, in 1979, the legendary Pete Rose arrived in Philadelphia as a free agent to take over at first base—his fourth different All-Star position. With Rose on board, the Phillies made another championship run in 1980. This time, they would not be denied.

Mike Schmidt was renowned for his slugging power but also showed better than average speed on the base paths, stealing 174 bases in his career.

MIKE SCHMIDT

SHORTSTOP · LARRY BOWA

Larry Bowa had great fielding instincts, a quick bat, lots of determination, and a fiery temper. Bowa ranks second in NL history in most career games played at shortstop (2,222). Known for his sure glove, Bowa said the secret to his fielding was his footwork. "If you have good footwork, you can get to the ball, set up, and get your body out of the way so you can make the throw," he explained. "I think that's the most important thing." After his playing days, Bowa managed the San Diego Padres and then the Phillies.

LARRY BOWA
SHORTSTOP

PHILADELPHIA
PHILLIES

STATS

Phillies seasons: 1970–81 (as player), 2001–04 (as manager)

Height: 5-foot-10

Weight: 155

- **2,191 career hits**

- **318 career stolen bases**

- **5-time All-Star**

- **2-time Gold Glove winner**

STEVE CARLTON

Everything came together in Philadelphia in 1980. Carlton earned
another Cy Young Award with a 24–9 record and 286 strikeouts, Schmidt
led the NL in home runs (48) and RBI (121), and right fielder Bake McBride
batted .309 to help the Phils capture their fourth NL East title in five
years. After defeating the Houston Astros in a hard-fought, five-game
NLCS, the Phillies faced off against the American League (AL) champion
Kansas City Royals in the World Series. The teams split the first four
games, each closely contested, before Philadelphia won the first world
championship in its 98-year existence with victories in Games 5 and 6. As
65,000 fans went wild in Veterans Stadium, an emotional McGraw said
simply, "This is the end of an incredible journey."

LEFT FIELDER · GREG LUZINSKI

In March 2004, Greg Luzinski pushed down the plunger that ignited the explosives that brought down old Veterans Stadium. Luzinski probably was given the honor because he had dented the walls and outfield seats at the stadium with so many hard-hit drives. During the 1970s, Luzinski teamed with Mike Schmidt to form the best power-hitting duo in the NL. Called "The Bull" because of his powerful arms and huge shoulders, Luzinski often seemed to run wild in left field as balls continually eluded his glove. But the Phillies relied on his offense more than his defense, and Luzinski usually came through in clutch situations.

GREG LUZINSKI
LEFT FIELDER

PHILADELPHIA
PHILLIES

STATS

Phillies seasons: 1970–80

Height: 6-foot-1

Weight: 225

• 307 career HR

• 675 career extra-base hits

• 3 seasons batting over .300

• 4-time All-Star

THE BIG FINISH

The Phillies won their first world championship in 1980, but the road to the title was not easy. Despite Mike Schmidt's league-leading 48 homers and 121 RBI, and Cy Young Award-winning pitching by Steve Carlton (who went 24–9 with a 2.34 ERA), the Phils spent very little time in first place in the NL East that year. It wasn't until the team won six straight games in the last week of the season that the Phillies were able to slip by the Montreal Expos and capture the division title. Winning the NLCS against the Houston Astros was no easy task, either. The Phils dropped two of the first three contests and were one loss away from being eliminated. Then they rallied in the 10th inning of both Games 4 and 5 in Houston to win their first pennant in 30 years. The World Series against the Kansas City Royals was just as tight; the first five games were all decided by one or two runs. The tension continued into the ninth inning of Game 6, when Pete Rose made a miraculous, bases-loaded catch in foul territory to help seal a 4–1 win and a Phillies championship at long last.

LENNY DYKSTRA

WILD TIMES

S chmidt, Carlton, and Rose would be around for one more pennant-winning season in 1983, but this time the Phillies were no match for the Baltimore Orioles in the World Series, and they lost in five games. During the rest of the 1980s, the club slowly sank in the NL East standings, finishing in the cellar in 1988 and 1989.

Several key trades led to a Philadelphia revival in the early 1990s. Among the newcomers were four unique players—outfielder Lenny Dykstra, first baseman John Kruk, starting pitcher Curt Schilling, and relief ace Mitch Williams. Of all those players, Dykstra, known as "Nails" for his hard-as-nails toughness, brought a particular intensity to the Phillies. "He has this winning glow about him that you can see even when he just walks through the clubhouse," said Phillies pitcher Roger McDowell. "I'm glad I don't have to play against him."

The other new Phillies had their own quirks. Kruk was a clubhouse prankster who kept the team loose and laughing.

Famed for his combination of hustle, aggression, and self-confidence, Lenny Dykstra represented the Phillies in the All-Star Game in 1990, 1994, and 1995.

Schilling had an intense "game face" that could wilt opposing batters as effectively as his fastball or slider could. Williams earned the nickname "Wild Thing" because he was not always able to control where his blazing fastballs would go.

Being different certainly worked for these Phillies. In 1993, they won 97 games, outdueled the Atlanta Braves in the NLCS, and roared into the World Series against the Toronto Blue Jays. Then, after six heart-stopping games, the Phils' thrilling run came to an abrupt end, thanks to a walk-off, three-run home run by Toronto outfielder Joe Carter in Game 6.

After that bitter defeat, the Phillies fell in the standings over the next few years. Then new manager Terry Francona and team officials began assembling a new lineup in the late 1990s, building around young players such as Gold Glove third baseman Scott Rolen, steady catcher Mike Lieberthal, and clutch-hitting right fielder Bobby Abreu. Still, the team continued to struggle on the field and at the ticket window. More than three million fans had packed Veterans Stadium during the 1993 season; by 2000, that number was cut in half. The need to economize led the Phillies to trade Schilling to the Arizona Diamondbacks in the middle of the 2000 season. Losing the longtime ace seemed to throw the club further into a funk, and the Phils finished the year in last place.

CENTER FIELDER · RICHIE ASHBURN

Richie Ashburn made reaching first base an art. He ranked first or second in the NL in hitting singles nine seasons and ranked first in walks four times. He was almost impossible to keep off base. During his 15-year career, he batted over .300 in 9 seasons and won 2 league batting titles. Ashburn was no slouch on defense either and is ranked by some baseball historians as one of the three best defensive center fielders of all time. While one generation of Phillies fans loved Ashburn as a player, two later generations adored him as a radio and television broadcaster for nearly 35 years.

RICHIE ASHBURN
CENTER FIELDER

PHILADELPHIA
PHILLIES

STATS

Phillies seasons: 1948–59

Height: 5-foot-10

Weight: 170

- **2,574 career hits**
- **.308 career BA**
- **5-time All-Star**
- **Baseball Hall of Fame inductee (1995)**

Francona was dismissed, and former Phillies shortstop Larry Bowa was brought in to energize the team and its fans.

Known for his intensity, Bowa quickly established a love-hate relationship with the players. He demanded that everyone perform with the same all-out passion he had during his All-Star playing career. "I'm sure to some of these guys, playing baseball is a hobby. To others, it's an occupation. We have to have 25 guys who think it's an occupation for us to succeed," Bowa explained. The new manager often seemed quick to criticize and slow to praise his players, but he found a way to motivate them. Led by Rolen, Abreu, and rookie shortstop Jimmy Rollins, the Phils made a run for the NL East title for most of the 2001 season before fading near the end.

After the Phillies slumped again in 2002, team management decided to shake things up a bit. Veteran first baseman Jim Thome, one of the top sluggers in the AL, joined the Phillies and immediately began powering baseballs out of Veterans Stadium, clubbing 47 dingers—the second-highest total in team history. Philadelphia also signed pitching ace Kevin Millwood away from Atlanta that season. Millwood proved his value immediately by hurling a no-hitter against the San Francisco Giants in late April, and the club seemed destined to make the playoffs until suffering another late-season fade.

CHASE UTLEY

CHAMPS AGAIN!

As they moved into a new home stadium—the state-of-the-art Citizens Bank Park—overlooking Philadelphia's Center City skyline, the Phillies were confident that 2004 would be a banner year. They started the season slowly, though, and even a late-season charge could not get them into the playoffs. At season's end, Bowa was fired and replaced

PHILLY HITTING STREAKS

Jimmy Rollins's 38-game hitting streak may go down in baseball history as the longest of all time. No, he didn't match Yankees great Joe DiMaggio's record of hitting safely in 56 straight games, but Rollins's streak lasted from August 2005 to April 2006. That's eight months, if you count the off-season. Long hitting streaks are a Phillies tradition. Outfielder Billy Hamilton, one of the stars of the hot-hitting 1894 Phillies, set the precedent when he hit safely in 36 straight games. Hamilton's teammate, outfielder Ed Delahanty, ran up an impressive 31-game streak in 1899, also among the best ever in NL history. More recent Phillies stars such as Richie Ashburn, Pete Rose, and Lenny Dykstra also have long hitting streaks in the team record book. But perhaps the most unusual hitting streak achievement of all time was recorded by Phillies outfielder Chuck Klein in 1930. Klein hit safely in 26 straight games in May and June. Then, a month later, he began another long streak that was also stopped after 26 games in early August. Overall, Klein hit safely in 135 of the team's 156 games in 1930, recorded 250 hits and 170 RBI, and compiled a spectacular .386 batting average.

RIGHT FIELDER · SAM THOMPSON

Whenever Sam Thompson settled into the batter's box, he struck fear into the hearts of pitchers and fielders. The 6-foot-2 Thompson crouched low at the plate, and as the pitch arrived, he jumped at it, scorching line drives to all parts of the field. Infielders, who wore very small gloves in those early days, often ducked to avoid his blasts. Using this style, Thompson compiled a career batting average of .331 and ranked as the most prolific home run hitter in the game until Babe Ruth appeared. Thompson's specialty was driving in runs; he still holds the major-league record for most RBI per game played.

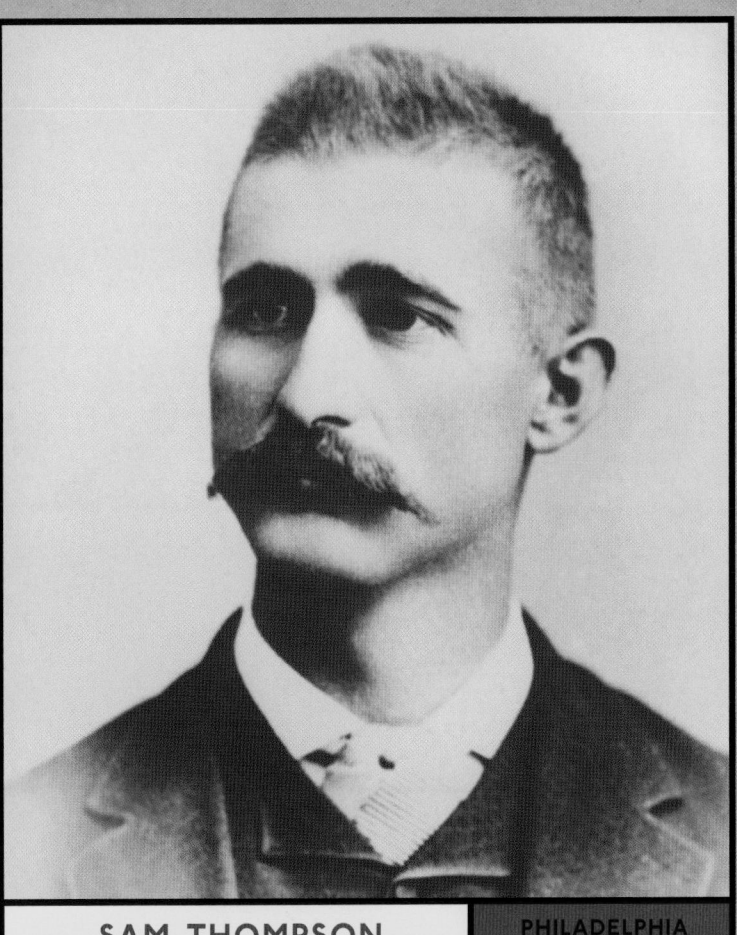

SAM THOMPSON
RIGHT FIELDER

PHILADELPHIA
PHILLIES

STATS

Phillies seasons: 1889–98

Height: 6-foot-2

Weight: 207

- **126 career HR**

- **1,305 career RBI**

- **161 career triples**

- **Baseball Hall of Fame inductee (1974)**

MANAGER · GENE MAUCH

Gene Mauch appeared in only 304 major-league games as a backup infielder. But he managed nearly 4,000 contests in Philadelphia, Montreal, Minnesota, and California. Mauch was a great strategist and one of the first NL managers to use the "double switch"—replacing a fielder at the same time he changed pitchers to move the pitcher lower in the batting order. "He was so far ahead of everyone and knew the rules better than anyone and used that to his advantage," said Phillies pitcher Dallas Green. Mauch's one regret was that he never managed a pennant winner in Philadelphia.

STATS

Phillies seasons as manager:
  1960–68

Managerial record: 1,902–2,037

GENE MAUCH
MANAGER

PHILADELPHIA
PHILLIES

by soft-spoken veteran manager Charlie Manuel. "We picked Charlie Manuel because he is a winning, championship-caliber manager," said Philadelphia general manager Ed Wade. "Charlie has the great ability to communicate with his players and build relationships with them, yet he demands excellence."

Manuel's easygoing but determined style helped bring out the best in the team's young, exciting players. Manuel's lineup featured an All-Star double-play combination—Rollins at shortstop and deceptively powerful Chase Utley at second base. Both players were graceful fielders, speedy runners, and steady hitters. The infield got even better in midseason when rookie Ryan Howard was called up to take over at first base. Howard bashed 22 home runs in only 88 games to earn the 2005 NL Rookie of the Year award. Led by Howard and Rollins—who finished the season with a 36-game hitting streak (which was extended to 38 games the next April)—the Phils finished the season 1 game shy of the NL Wild Card berth.

The Phillies barely missed the playoffs again in 2006. Howard made major headlines that year, breaking the club home run record by slamming 58

JIMMY ROLLINS

dingers and also driving in 149 runs to earn the 2006 NL MVP award. The excitement in Philadelphia continued to build in 2007. That year, Rollins earned his own MVP trophy by leading the Phillies on an incredible late-season charge that carried them past the fading New York Mets to the NL East title and their first postseason appearance in 14 years. Even a quick playoff exit at the hands of the Colorado Rockies couldn't dampen the enthusiasm of the Philadelphia faithful, who were eager for the 2008 season to begin.

The fans' optimism was rewarded when the 2008 Phils got off to a hot start. They faded in midseason but used a strong finish to win the NL East for the second straight year. During the season, Philadelphia's high-scoring offense was the key to victory. In the playoffs, the club's pitchers took over. Lefty Cole Hamels, right-hander Brett Myers, and closer Brad Lidge shut down the Milwaukee Brewers in the first round and the Los Angeles Dodgers in the NLCS. The Phillies then capped a season to remember by quickly dispatching the upstart AL champion Tampa Bay Rays in the World Series to bring the championship trophy back to Philadelphia for the first time since 1980. "For all these years, the

2008 WORLD SERIES

WAITING TO WIN

On October 27, 2008, fans packed Citizens Bank Park, hoping to watch their Phillies—ahead three games to one in the World Series against the Tampa Bay Rays—win Game 5 and capture the second world championship in team history. Smart fans brought umbrellas with them that night, as a cold, steady rain fell throughout the game. By the top of the sixth inning, the Phils were ahead 2–1, but the field was nearly unplayable. Players were slipping everywhere, and batters could barely see balls coming toward home plate. Still, the Rays managed to scratch out a tying run in the sixth. It was then that

umpires decided to suspend the game and pick up again once the rain had stopped. Nearly 45 hours later, the longest inning in World Series history resumed. The Phillies scored quickly to go up 3–2, but the Rays tied the contest in the seventh inning. Philadelphia scored a fourth run, and second baseman Chase Utley helped preserve the lead by cutting down speedy Tampa Bay runner Jason Bartlett in a bang-bang play at the plate. One inning later, at 9:58 P.M. on October 29, closer Brad Lidge struck out Rays outfielder Eric Hinske, and the Phillies were world champs.

PHILLIES

[43]

Ryan Howard became one of the richest baseball stars when he signed a 5-year, $125-million contract extension with Philadelphia in 2010.

STANLEY

RYAN HOWARD

ROY HALLADAY

Roy Halladay made history in 2010 by becoming just the second pitcher ever to throw a no-hitter in the playoffs, blanking the Cincinnati Reds in Game 1 of the first round.

part of playing here that upset me the most was that I was always home in October, watching somebody else celebrate," said Rollins. "But this year, *we* get to celebrate."

The highflying Phillies roared to another NL pennant and World Series in 2009. This time, however, they came up short to the star-laden Yankees, who took the series in six games. In 2010, behind newly obtained ace starter Roy Halladay, Philadelphia came just two victories short of a third straight pennant, winning its division but falling to the San Francisco Giants in a six-game NLCS. Although Philadelphia fans were disappointed by the loss, they took solace in the fact that their Phillies were now clearly a baseball heavyweight. With a pitching staff headed by Halladay, Hamels, and newly obtained Cliff Lee, and with an offense featuring the power of Howard and Utley and the speed of Rollins and center fielder Shane "The Flyin' Hawaiian" Victorino, the Phils had designs on more world titles in the seasons to come.

Like their home city, the Philadelphia Phillies can boast of a long and impressive history, with some of the greatest stars in the game having worn Phillies red over a span of nearly 130 years. Today's Phillies—having settled into a beautiful new home and recently basked in World Series glory—are looking to build on that history one more championship at a time.

PHILLIES

INDEX